ASCD | arias

BUILDING A MATH-POSITIVE CULTURE

How to Support Great Math Teaching in Your School

Cathy L. **SEELEY**

ASCD

Alexandria, VA USA

NCSM
LEADERSHIP IN MATHEMATICS EDUCATION
NETWORK
COMMUNICATE
SUPPORT
MOTIVATE

Aurora, CO USA

NCTM | NATIONAL COUNCIL OF TEACHERS OF MATHEMATICS

Reston, VA USA

www.ascd.org
books@ascd.org

www.mathedleadership.org
office@mathedleadership.org

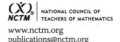
www.nctm.org
publications@nctm.org

Published simultaneously by ASCD, 1703 N. Beauregard Street, Alexandria, VA 22311, the National Council of Supervisors of Mathematics, 2851 S. Parker Road #1210, Aurora, CO 80014, and the National Council of Teachers of Mathematics, 1906 Association Drive, Reston, VA 20191.

Printed in the United States of America. ASCD publications present a variety of viewpoints. The views expressed or implied in this book should not be interpreted as official positions of the Association.

ASCD®, ASCD LEARN TEACH LEAD®, ASCD ARIAS™, and ANSWERS YOU NEED FROM VOICES YOU TRUST® are trademarks owned by ASCD and may not be used without permission. All other referenced trademarks are the property of their respective owners.

PAPERBACK ISBN: 978-1-4166-2246-8   ASCD product #SF116068

Also available as an e-book (see Books in Print for the ISBNs).

Library of Congress Cataloging-in-Publication Data

Names: Seeley, Cathy L.
Title: Building a math-positive culture : how to support great math teaching in your school / Cathy L. Seeley.
Description: Alexandria, Virginia, USA : ASCD, 2016. | Includes bibliographical references and index.
Identifiers: LCCN 2016004940 | ISBN 9781416622468 (pbk. : alk. paper)
Subjects: LCSH: Mathematics--Study and teaching (Elementary) -Handbooks,
    manuals, etc. | Mathematics teachers--Training of--Handbooks, manuals, etc.
Classification: LCC QA135.6 .S445 2016 | DDC 510.71/2--dc23 LC record available at http://lccn.loc.gov/2016004940

24 23 22 21 20 19 18 17 16   1 2 3 4 5 6 7 8 9 10

ASCD | arias

BUILDING A MATH-POSITIVE CULTURE

How to Support Great Math Teaching in Your School

Want to earn a free ASCD Arias e-book?
Your opinion counts! Please take 2–3 minutes to give
us your feedback on this publication. All survey
respondents will be entered into a drawing to
win an ASCD Arias e-book.

Please visit
www.ascd.org/ariasfeedback

Thank you!

Introduction

It seems that we see headlines almost daily reporting some change in educational policy at the national or state level. A leader who wants to see improved student achievement in mathematics may not know where to start. Will the standards change? What state accountability measures should drive our efforts? Do the experts agree on how to improve mathematics teaching and learning? Forces outside your school or district may seem to offer little in terms of a firm foundation on which to build programmatic changes. But a leader can still make a difference, even in this seemingly volatile environment. The nature of an effective mathematics program remains consistent in many ways, even as we need to make adjustments for the changing world our students face. A leader working with a group of committed teachers can support effective mathematics teaching and learning in several important ways, from providing a boost for a program already showing signs of success to instigating a more substantial turnaround.

Preparing students for their future calls for fresh thinking about mathematics teaching and learning. Many in the general population don't like math and consider it to be hard. While they may see the usefulness of basic arithmetic (although that skill is becoming less necessary as technological devices become more accessible), they may not see the use for other types of mathematics, such as algebra. And many believe that math ability is something a person is born with—or without. Yet, quantitative skills are becoming more and more important for dealing with the pervasive use of data in our daily lives. The need for a renewed vision of vibrant, relevant mathematics has never been greater. And the need to sell the public—and even teachers—on the importance of broad and deep mathematics education presents not only a significant challenge but also a great opportunity for leaders.

Shifting the mathematics program in a school or school system is an ambitious task that can yield huge benefits for students. Leaders can effectively drive such an effort using some key tools, depending on their particular role and job responsibilities. They can build collective support around a new vision of mathematics, provide essential resources and support for teachers, and implement or encourage policies that nurture and sustain long-term improvement.

This brief book offers an overview of what an effective and successful mathematics program might look like at any level in the K–12 system, as well as examples of what a leader can do to support support that goal. We will consider the needs and abilities of the students we serve, the nature of the mathematics we want them to learn, the kinds of classrooms where that learning can best take place, the culture of schools where such classrooms thrive, and the first steps in a process for creating those schools.

To further explore how to create and support math classrooms focused on meaning and deep understanding, see my companion volume for teachers, *Making Sense of Math* (Seeley, 2016).

What Does It Mean to Be Good at Math?

Mathematics seems to be unique in the attitudes it brings out in people. Many adults dislike mathematics, and many believe they are just not born to be "math people." Unfortunately, that harmful belief seems to have been passed on to many students. In truth, there is absolutely no evidence to support the idea that mathematical ability is based on a "math gene." Mathematics has many dimensions, and there are many ways to be good at math. We now know that anyone of average intelligence can learn mathematics if we teach it in appropriately engaging ways. Emerging work on the nature of intelligence and how people learn mathematics is helping educators reexamine old assumptions and beliefs about what it takes to be good at math and even what it means to be smart in general.

A Growth Mindset of Intelligence

Historically, two bodies of thought have dominated both research and public perception about intelligence. In the groundbreaking book *Mindset*, Carol Dweck (2006) describes two mindsets about intelligence—a *fixed mindset* and a *growth mindset*. A fixed mindset represents the point of view that intelligence is a fixed quantity determined solely by a person's genes. People with a fixed mindset about intelligence believe that every person is born as smart as they will ever be. A growth mindset, on the other hand, represents the idea that genetic makeup is only the starting point. People with a growth mindset about intelligence believe that, while a person may be born with certain genes, their life experiences and a variety of influences from family, society, and the media can impact how smart that person may become. A growing body of hard scientific research supports the idea that intelligence is, in fact, malleable, not fixed. From brain scans of people working on difficult problems, we have learned that the brain can grow new neural connections— new synapses—that form the basis of a person's intelligence. Dweck believes that a person's mindset affects not only how well that person will do in school, but also how she will function in relationships, the workplace, and everyday life.

The Impact of Mindset on Learning and Teaching

Students who have come to adopt a fixed mindset about intelligence, even if they don't use those words, believe they are as smart now as they're ever going to be. When they encounter difficult math problems they don't immediately know how to solve, they're likely to think, "Well, I guess I've hit my limit. I must not be smart enough to solve this kind of problem." And they give up. An unwillingness to try a hard problem is pervasive among American teenagers, reaching epidemic proportions by the time students leave high school. This unwillingness to try and lack of persistence cross all levels of academic success, affecting students who are successful (perhaps even in an accelerated track) as well as students who struggle to learn. Too many students have come to believe that they either have reached or will soon reach the limit of how smart they are. Their fixed mindset has become entrenched as a fundamental belief.

On the other hand, students who understand that intelligence is not fixed but can grow may approach a tough problem by thinking, "Wow. This seems like a really hard problem. I may have to work on it a while. It may take some time." A growth mindset equips students to be willing to tackle hard problems and persevere until they arrive at a solution.

Probably at least as important as a student's mindset is a teacher's mindset. If a teacher believes that students are limited in terms of how far they can go, the teacher is likely to set low expectations and potentially fail to adequately challenge students. A teacher's mindset about intelligence affects plans for daily teaching as well as interactions with students during class. Both teachers and students can benefit from learning about a growth mindset and the potential to become smarter as they tackle challenging mathematics.

Teaching About a Growth Mindset

Learning about the nature of intelligence, including the power of a growth mindset, and learning how to share this knowledge with students should be part of every teacher's professional education. Some programs, like the Academic

Youth Development program (The Charles A. Dana Center at the University of Texas at Austin, 2016) have shown that we can be successful teaching students about intelligence, learning, and even brain research as part of their instructional program.

Understanding a growth mindset can change how we plan and implement our mathematics teaching. In the book *Mathematical Mindsets*, Jo Boaler (2015) makes a beautiful case for helping students learn about a growth mindset and making some shifts in how we teach. She also reminds us about the value of embracing mistakes. From what we've learned about how intelligence can be affected by experience, we now know that not only is making mistakes normal, it may actually represent an important component to learning and growing intelligence.

Being Smart in Math

It's a common misconception that someone who's good at math is someone who can compute quickly and accurately. But mathematics is a broad discipline, and there are many ways to be smart in math. Some students are good at seeing relationships among numbers, quantities, or objects. Others may be creative problem solvers, able to come up with nonroutine ways to approach an unfamiliar problem. Still others may be good at visually representing relationships or problems or translating from one representation to another—from a graph to a table, from an equation to a graph, or from a word problem to a pictorial model, for example. All of these students—and others—should have the opportunity to access mathematics from different entry points and become successful math students. A comprehensive mathematics program not only makes room for and nurtures all kinds of smart students, it also creates opportunities for students to expand the strengths they have to help them access other dimensions of mathematics. And it offers such opportunities to all students—even those who may be disenfranchised or disengaged with mathematics, often hidden in remedial programs or special classes.

What Should a Good Mathematics Program Look Like?

The National Research Council defines *mathematical proficiency* as consisting of five strands: Understanding (comprehending concepts), Computing (performing procedures accurately, efficiently, and flexibly), Applying (using math to formulate and solve problems), Reasoning (explaining and justifying using logic), and Engaging (making sense of math, seeing it as useful and doable, and being willing to do the work) (Findell & Swafford, 2002). It's important for a school's mathematics program to address all of these elements in order to adequately prepare students to use mathematics in their future.

The Building Blocks for Your Math Program

When I was in elementary school, several decades ago, all students took the Iowa Test of Basic Skills, a norm-referenced standardized test designed to assign a percentile rank to each child. A student's mathematics score on the test was reported in three categories: Concepts, Computation, and Problem Solving. Today, even in an era of new standards and performance assessments, our priorities in mathematics are not that different from what they were in the mid–20th century. Students still need to understand concepts, perform computations, and solve problems. Each of these three components is essential in order for students to function as mathematical thinkers who can use what they know.

Concepts. Understanding what numbers and operations represent, being able to see and analyze relationships among objects or quantities, and noticing and generalizing from patterns are all elements of the kind of conceptual understanding our students need.

Computation. Even with the increasing potential and availability of technology, students still need to know some facts and be able to perform computational procedures, although not necessarily to the extent that they once did. Mental math, including reasonable fact recall, may be more important than ever, but we might want to seriously consider how long a divisor is necessary in long division or how ugly a denominator students need to be subjected to in computing with fractions. In today's technologically driven world, relatively few situations arise in which we still need to perform such computations with a pencil and paper.

Problem solving. Understanding and computational skill can only help students so much if they cannot apply what they know to solve a wide range of problems, including problems that may be unfamiliar to them.

Today, we know more than ever before how concepts, computation, and problem solving can be developed with lasting understanding and fluency. We also know how the three elements interconnect and support each other. If any of the three are missing in a program, the program will not adequately prepare students for the future. And students who are seriously deficient in any of the three elements are not likely to be able to use what they know in any meaningful way. Standards in most states, including the Common Core State Standards for Mathematics, make a deliberate attempt to balance these three elements.

Developing Fluency in a Technological World

Many standards and curriculum programs call for students to develop fluency with fact recall and computation, and this is a reasonable and important priority in a mathematics program. But we need to be careful not to equate fluency with the ability to quickly complete timed tests on fact recall or computation. Rather, fluency means that a student can accurately, efficiently, and flexibly apply a fact or procedure when called for without having to go through a process of figuring it out (National Council of Teachers of Mathematics, 2014b). Fluency builds on conceptual understanding and depends on a broad and deep knowledge of mathematics, including connecting ideas from different parts of mathematics and being able to reason and justify when performing computations. We might think of a student as fluent with certain multiplication facts, for example, if he knows that $4 \times 6 = 24$ without resorting to a strategy like doubling and halving or a cumbersome method like counting or drawing a picture. Such techniques can be helpful when learning facts, but eventually we want students to move past these methods to internalize what they know so that their strategies don't slow them down when solving problems.

We should also consider that the goal to develop fluency should not keep a student from progressing past a computational roadblock to take on worthwhile problems that require thinking and reasoning well beyond computational competence. The appropriate use of calculators can help students address challenging, interesting, and relevant problems that require thinking and creative problem solving without getting stalled by computational gaps or by the time it takes to do complicated calculations. In fact, working on such rich problems, even with a calculator, can sometimes motivate students to address their computational gaps (Seeley, 2015).

The Allure of Timed Tests

One common trap leaders may fall into is thinking that a schoolwide (or districtwide) focus on fast fact recall or computational excellence is an appropriate starting point for changing a school's math culture. Unfortunately, such a narrow focus, especially when paired with the pressure of time, can lead to exactly the opposite result that leaders are trying to achieve. We repeatedly find that the use of timed tests is at least as harmful for some students as it may be helpful for others, in addition to incorrectly communicating what mathematics is all about (Boaler 2015; Seeley 2015). In fact, many students develop lasting negative attitudes about mathematics and about themselves as math students from their experience with timed tests, and those attitudes undermine their confidence and willingness to tackle any mathematical problem. Leaders can play a key role in helping teachers keep their eyes on a broader, more comprehensive vision of what mathematics proficiency looks like.

The Threads That Connect the Pieces

While addressing the content of a mathematics program may be the central focus of many improvement efforts, we need to keep in mind that the most important outcome should be for students to be able to think mathematically. Being able to connect math they know with math that might be useful in a particular situation calls for deeply rooted mathematical habits of mind. Students—and their teachers—need to be able to understand how mathematical ideas relate to each other, to notice and generalize patterns, and to understand the logic, reasoning, and underlying structure that make mathematics a powerful tool. In particular, they need to not only see that mathematics *can* make sense, they need to come to expect that everything they do in math *should* make sense. This expectation should drive teachers and students to understand what they do and what they learn as they dig ever deeper and ask more questions whenever something doesn't make sense.

What Else Is Important?

In today's rapidly changing world, the ability to adapt what we know to new situations has become a critical skill. Many of the job situations our students will eventually face don't even exist today. If these young people are to be adequately prepared for their future, they need a robust set of thinking skills and abilities beyond traditional mathematics concepts and skills. Many states and organizations have identified the kinds of skills students need to be ready for college and the workplace, such as the ability to reason, gather evidence to back up a point of view, interpret data, generate new ideas, collaborate with others, share their thinking and communicate with others about theirs, use technological tools appropriately, and be willing to tackle and persevere through problems they've never encountered before. Many of these cross-disciplinary skills echo what mathematics experts have been calling for since the late 20th century, and they should be reflected in an effective math program.

A Note About High School

Most states' mathematics standards today include a streamlined set of expectations, with a few identified priorities for each grade level through grade 8. At the high school level, however, standards for courses labeled as Algebra I, Geometry, and Algebra II continue to be overly packed with content, at least some of which may not be relevant or necessary for many students. With a few notable exceptions, content in these courses has changed very little over the years. A few programs have developed innovative ways to incorporate some relevant and important topics like statistics and mathematical modeling into Algebra I, Geometry, and Algebra II courses. But more often, the courses tend to focus on abstract rules and procedures, leaving little time for topics that might serve more students well. Once designed for a relatively small group of students headed toward mathematics-intensive majors at the university level, these three courses have now been retrofitted in an attempt to respond to the very real need for more mathematics for all students. Unfortunately, these particular courses are not always the best fit for students who may be headed in a variety of directions after high school. Nevertheless, teachers are expected to teach to the standards they're given, so it's important to do everything possible to make the content students learn as accessible and relevant as possible.

Some schools and a few states have made the shift to an integrated course structure for high school mathematics, building on the approach already in place in our K–8 standards and similar to the organization of secondary mathematics courses in essentially every other country in the world. I applaud this move toward a more blended and relevant approach to high school mathematics. A well-designed, integrated program generally incorporates content from several strands of mathematics, such as algebra, geometry, statistics, finance, and discrete math, and it emphasizes the development of flexible and comprehensive problem-solving skills. These new courses often emphasize the use of mathematics to model real situations. Simply combining content areas, however, does not ensure that a program is well designed. It's important to build courses around the coherent development of topics over the years and to consider how the different threads of mathematics can be used together to build stronger understanding and more powerful content development than would be possible in separate courses.

Regrettably, with no national agreement on what content should be included in each year of an integrated high school mathematics program, there isn't much consistency in instructional materials for such programs, and accountability tests often fall short in accommodating an integrated approach. Perhaps one day we will, as a nation, come to a consensus on how to organize an integrated high school mathematics program that meets the needs of all students. And perhaps one day, accountability tests will be designed that support every school that moves toward this more rational, relevant, and useful approach to educating our high school students. In the meantime, we can continue to work to ensure that every student has an opportunity to learn relevant, challenging, useful mathematics, whatever the names of particular courses might be.

How Do I Recognize, Support, and Evaluate Effective Math Teaching?

Regardless of the structure of a program, the materials used, or any innovation a school implements, the most important aspect of students' mathematics continues to be the interactions between teacher and students.

The Importance of Teachers

Teaching the kind of mathematics described here calls for a teacher to deeply understand mathematics well beyond the grade level being taught. Professional recommendations call for secondary teachers to know mathematics at the level of a college major in mathematics, and for elementary teachers to have significant coursework or professional learning that helps them understand the deep foundations of the number system (including the meanings of basic operations), concepts of measurement and geometry (including spatial reasoning), and basic notions of statistics and algebra (Mathematical Association of America, 2015; National Council of Teachers of Mathematics & Council for the Accreditation of Educator Preparation, 2012). Teachers at all grade levels should also have an understanding of mathematical topics unique to K–12 education and not necessarily found in most university math majors, including critical connecting concepts such as proportionality and equivalence.

For leaders, this means that either every teacher should have a strong mathematical background or the school should be organized in a way that allows only those teachers who have a strong background in mathematics to teach math. If it's not possible to hire (or train) well-prepared mathematics teachers for every classroom at the elementary level, for example, then the school should seriously consider departmentalizing mathematics or having it taught by math specialists. Even children in the early grades need to be taught by teachers who both know and like mathematics. The foundation children build in the primary grades—especially in the areas of number sense and operation sense—is essential for all the rest of their mathematical development. It's foolish to invest only in mathematical preparation for teachers who teach the upper grades if students are going to arrive at those grades with misconceptions and misunderstandings that are difficult, if not impossible, to overcome.

The Teaching Students Need

Beyond teachers' mathematical knowledge, it's important to ensure that mathematics teachers are effective in terms of their day-to-day instructional practice. Teachers need to understand how to choose relevant, worthwhile tasks just a bit beyond what students may already know and think they can do—tasks that engage students in meaningful struggle as they work toward the mathematical outcomes of the lesson. They need to understand how to structure classroom discussions around student thinking and how to build on students' mistakes for deeper understanding. And they need to know ways to formatively assess what students are learning on a regular basis in order to adjust their teaching or offer appropriate interventions. Effective mathematics teaching may look very different from effective teaching in other disciplines. It's not reasonable to expect that strategies that work well for helping students become readers, for example, can automatically be transferred as effective strategies for helping students become mathematically proficient thinkers and problem solvers.

Mathematics teaching today should involve much more student discussion about their work on rich, worthwhile problems than typically found in the teacher-centered, lecture-based classrooms many of us experienced as students (National Council of Teachers of Mathematics, 2011, 2014a). Unfortunately, many classrooms today continue to rely on this limiting model of mathematics teaching—telling students what they should remember and guiding them through practice on mechanical skills for certain types of problems. Fortunately, more and more teachers are learning how to organize their classrooms differently, focusing on engaging problems that allow students to productively struggle toward understanding, and using students' discussion of their work as a platform for learning the mathematics they need.

The Role of Technology in Teaching

Computers, calculators, and other technological tools are important resources that can enhance mathematics instruction if used in appropriate ways. However, a computer program cannot replace a teacher. The kind of rich, engaging, productive discussions needed to help students learn to think and solve problems generally cannot occur without the facilitation of a skilled teacher. While the capabilities of technological resources continue to evolve, it's not realistic to consider replacing an ineffective teacher with a computer as a long-term solution. Rather than investing in more computers, a leader would be wise to invest in hiring knowledgeable, well-qualified teachers and in strengthening the knowledge and skills of current teachers.

What to Look For

Classrooms that focus on developing mathematically proficient students tend to share several characteristics. These characteristics may be described in slightly different ways (Chapin, O'Connor, & Anderson, 2013; National Council of Teachers of Mathematics, 2014a; Smith & Stein, 2011), but essentially they involve the following:

- Organizing lessons around carefully selected **tasks** that involve worthwhile mathematics, challenge students, and support productive struggle toward meaningful learning
- Facilitated mathematical **discussion** among students
- Well-designed **questions** that elicit student thinking
- A commitment to building **fluency** on conceptual **understanding**
- Explicit **connections** between the activities of a lesson and the intended mathematical learning

I sometimes think of this kind of teaching as "upside-down teaching" (Seeley, 2014, 2016). Instead of taking a traditional approach to mathematics teaching, in which students are presented with a procedure and then assigned one or more word problems to apply the just-learned technique, in upside-down teaching, a teacher starts by presenting students with a problem to wrestle with and uses classroom discussion about students' work as a platform for addressing the intended mathematics of the lesson. Upside-down teaching involves a shift from an "I-We-You" model of teaching (*I* explain, *we* work together through guided practice, *you* work on your own) to a "You-We-I" model (*you* work on a problem, *we* discuss your work, *I* make sure you learn the mathematics). While an I-We-You approach, sometimes called "gradual release of responsibility," may be advocated for some disciplines, such as reading (Fisher & Frey, 2013; Pearson & Gallagher, 1983), it has not been shown to be effective for developing mathematical proficiency that includes the development of thinking skills and the ability to tackle problems that may not fit a particular format. On the other hand, we see growing consensus in support of a teaching model that involves students productively struggling on engaging tasks and discussing their work as a vehicle for deep, lasting, and usable learning (Chapin et al., 2013; National Council of Teachers of Mathematics, 2014a; Smith & Stein, 2011).

Professional Learning Opportunities

Teaching in this way calls for a much stronger and deeper background in mathematics than preparing a lecture involving minimal student interaction. Teachers need to know enough mathematics to deal with unexpected ideas and approaches students might offer and to identify potential misconceptions before they become habits. Some teachers may need considerable coursework or long-term, in-depth professional development focused on expanding mathematics content knowledge while also learning how to teach differently. Regardless of their individual background and experience, all teachers can benefit from ongoing professional learning to refine their teaching practice and increase their own mathematical understanding.

Bringing together teachers from multiple grades or school levels can be an effective structure for some types of professional development opportunities. While it's often useful for teachers to target their professional learning to their particular grade-level content, some unexpected benefits can arise by having teachers from multiple grade levels work together on a common theme or topic, such as proportionality. This important connecting topic evolves from early elementary grades through middle school and well into high school. Yet few teachers realize the full range of how proportionality develops or are aware of what related experiences their students may have had before or may see in the future. A workshop or series of learning opportunities on proportional relationships for K–12 teachers can help everyone strengthen their understanding of this critical topic. In the process, elementary teachers will see where basic multiplicative relationships lead, and secondary teachers will gain insights into the building blocks that serve as a basis for linear functions. Similar opportunities might be built around how the distributive property develops across the grades or the nature and representation of equivalence, for example.

Administrative Support

Beyond helping teachers expand their content and pedagogical knowledge, leaders can also support teachers by carefully examing the policies they enact that affect teachers. Some well-intentioned practices may actually interfere with a professional teacher doing what's right for students.

In particular, requirements to follow rigid pacing guides or teach from scripted lessons keep teachers from having adequate instructional time or flexibility to "finish teaching." Far too often, teachers who know their students could benefit from more instructional time on a particular concept or skill choose to move on to the next lesson anyway. They feel (or are told that) their job is to "cover" a prescribed list of content. One of the most powerful things a leader can do is give permission for teachers to finish teaching, at least in terms of the highest-priority concepts or skills in a grade or course. Teachers should work together to identify a few major priorities for each grade level or course, and then do whatever is necessary to help students succeed at—finish learning—those priorities. Since it's not possible to provide extended time for every concept, skill, or problem at every level, this may mean that other topics get less attention. It's important to communicate this kind of information with teachers at the next level so that they can determine whether additional attention might be necessary on those topics. But the alternative—covering all of the content in a superficial or rushed fashion—leads to shallow learning that doesn't last and won't help students solve the complex problems they're likely to see in the future, whether as a performance task on a test or in their lives outside of school.

Likewise, well-intentioned schoolwide practices like the required use of timed tests or special daily activities that reinforce a single aspect of mathematics should be carefully reviewed. In some cases, schools have devised positive and successful ways of supporting mathematical proficiency with schoolwide initiatives. Publicly posted "Problems of the Week," for example, might call for creative thinking or cross-disciplinary applications of mathematics. Such problems, perhaps offered at different levels, could positively reinforce mathematical thinking and problem solving. The required use of timed tests, on the other hand, is often a negative reinforcement of students' perceptions about the nature of mathematics and can send the wrong message about what it means to be good at math. And practices like benchmark testing—administering frequent practice or readiness tests throughout the year in preparation for the year-end accountability test—can sometimes turn into an unreasonable burden on teachers and an interruption to learning for students, especially if tests are given frequently or if they require extensive class time. For any practice or policy, it's a good idea to consider the cost/benefit ratio. Are the results likely to benefit students, and will the results be worth the cost of the time and energy required?

Front-Line Support

One important resource that can potentially help teachers the most is the use of math specialists and math coaches. Math specialists might actually teach mathematics or might support teachers who have weaker math backgrounds. Math coaches can work with teachers one-on-one, sometimes doing shared teaching or demonstration teaching, sometimes observing teaching, and sometimes consulting with a teacher and working together toward the teacher's goals. In whatever way the role of a specialist or coach is defined for a particular school, the most important advantage of having such resource people available is that teachers with a responsibility to teach mathematics have someone who can work with them—someone who is knowledgeable and current about mathematics and the most effective ways to teach it.

Professional learning communities can offer another way to help teachers continue to grow and refine their teaching. Working together with colleagues, professional teachers can invest their time where it makes the most difference—focusing on student work and discussing together how to improve learning through what teachers do in the classroom. But like any other good idea, professional learning communities can sometimes deteriorate into a superficial exercise, becoming little more than glorified faculty meetings with checklists of who came to which meetings and what was discussed. Effectively used, however, a professional learning community can become a powerful vehicle that can elevate the quality of mathematics teaching and learning throughout a school.

Evaluation of Mathematics Teaching

Teacher evaluation is an evolving process. The Every Student Succeeds Act of 2015 opened the door for more varied and professional processes for evaluating the effectiveness of teachers in all subject areas. Whatever criteria, processes, or tools are used, it's important to evaluate teachers of mathematics in ways that recognize and reward the kind of teaching that builds comprehensive mathematical proficiency. This means not expecting that students should sit quietly in their seats listening to a teacher or working on individual work. And it means holding high expectations for teachers to be knowledgeable about mathematics and how to teach it, including being skilled at facilitating classroom discussions, asking purposeful questions that draw out student thinking, helping students make sense of what they're learning, and equipping them to solve a wide range of problems.

One important element in any teacher evaluation system, especially in terms of classroom observation, is working together with the teacher to identify goals in advance and to debrief after the observation. It can be productive to meet with the teacher beforehand to discuss what the teacher is trying to accomplish and hopes for how the class will unfold. This kind of meeting invites teachers to be important partners in the evaluation process, reinforcing their professionalism and helping them make the best use possible of the information gained during an observation and the resulting evaluation.

What's Working and What's Not?

In order for a leader to determine what level of action might be helpful or necessary to support a math-positive culture in a school or district, it's important to take a look at whether the current program reflects appropriate goals for teaching and learning and how well the program achieves those goals.

Components of a High-Quality Math Program

Effective mathematics programs don't all look alike in terms of details like which materials are used or how classes are scheduled. But they generally share a culture that values mathematics as a subject that's vital for students' future success, celebrates meaningful accomplishments in mathematics teaching and learning, and works to serve all students. In a school with a high-quality mathematics program, every student has the opportunity to learn challenging, worthwhile, engaging, and relevant mathematics, regardless of a student's past experience or special label (ELL, SPED, ED, etc.). A high-quality mathematics program gives every student the opportunity to become a "math person." The seven components below offer a possible foundation for taking a closer look at what's working in your school's math program and what areas could improve:

- **Content**—The program's mathematical content addresses a blend of computation, concepts, and problem solving for all students.
- **Habits of Mind**—The program emphasizes mathematical thinking and processes for all students, with a focus on students learning to think mathematically and make sense of what they do.
- **Teachers**—All students are taught by a professional teacher who likes mathematics and knows mathematics deeply, with an ongoing investment in helping all teachers reflect on their practice and

continue to develop as experts in school mathematics and effective teaching practices.

+ **Teaching and Learning**—All students have opportunities to productively struggle with engaging problems as they discuss, justify, and question their own and each other's work and learn from mistakes to develop mathematical proficiency.

+ **Assessment**—Effective formative assessment strategies allow teachers to monitor and help students improve their learning on a daily basis, and summative assessment strategies complement instruction, rather than interrupt it, and maintain a focus on the goals, priorities, and values of the program.

+ **Teacher Evaluation**—Leaders use multidimensional teacher evaluation systems that reward instruction that helps students develop proficiency as mathematical thinkers, even if that instruction may look different from effective instruction in other subject areas.

+ **Outreach**—School leaders and teachers involve and communicate with families and the broader community with respect to the mathematics program, including sharing—or even working together to determine—the purposes, assumptions, and intended outcomes of the program and offering suggestions for what families and the community can do to help all students become mathematically proficient thinkers.

Agreement on the Goal

A good starting point for taking a look at a school's math program is to work together to identify a broad goal for the program. Such a task would ideally involve all teachers and school administrators and possibly other stakeholders, such as parents or even students (or recent graduates). A school faculty, group of teachers in a grade level or department, or expanded group of stakeholders might consider a task such as the following as a first step in looking at the overall school program in mathematics:

> Write one sentence that describes the kind of mathematics students should know and be able to do when they graduate from high school.

The task is not to write a list of bullets, but rather a broad yet concise statement that captures what someone considers most important. After participants have a couple of minutes to write individually, they can share their sentences in groups of two to five. Each group can discuss and negotiate, if necessary, to create a shared sentence that captures the highlights of the group's thinking. The process could even be expanded to a larger group, eventually arriving at a statement that represents the collective thinking of the grade level, department, or school.

Keeping in mind the important end result of their work—the proficiency of a high school graduate—can help teachers focus on the big picture, even as they face pacing guides and checklists of specific standards, objectives, or test specifications on a daily basis. And when other stakeholders are involved, such as parents, graduates, higher education faculty, or community members, the process of agreeing on a broad long-term goal can set the stage for productive discussions about potentially delicate or controversial issues.

Such a task can be productive for any level, from elementary through high school, and can be beneficial for work across levels as the basis for a shared professional development experience. Elementary or middle schools might consider a follow-up task to describe what students should know or be able to do when they finish the highest grade at that school. Teachers within a specific grade level or course could discuss what part of the overall goal should be their responsibility.

Evidence of Success

It can be tempting to try to judge the effectiveness of a program simply by looking at scores on the state accountability test. But test scores offer just one type of data, and they can mask underlying issues, both positive and negative. It is also important to look at data about other parts of a math program, such as what content is being taught, how content is being taught and assessed, and the broader school context within which the program operates. Gathering a variety of types of data or evidence will help leaders obtain a more complete picture of their school's mathematics program, as described in the data-gathering tasks that follow. Note that each task identifies which components of a high-quality math program it targets.

Data on student learning. Test scores represent an important source of data and a reasonable starting point. However, an accountability test that is limited in scope by a single-answer, multiple-choice format is unlikely to address deep conceptual understanding or authentic problem solving. Recent innovations in accountability testing have resulted in some states now using tests that include extended performance tasks over multiple standards as well as items that target mathematical practices and thinking skills. However, such tests are not yet used in every state. It's important to consider how well your state's test aligns with the goals and priorities of your program.

> **Task 1 (Assessment)**: Determine how well the accountability test measures mathematical thinking; in-depth, open-ended problem solving; mathematical processes and practices; and connections across mathematics topics and skills.

Information beyond test scores to consider includes the graduation rate (for high schools) and how it may have changed in recent years. Student grades are an important factor at any level, as is student performance on department or grade-level tests. And teachers' records of formative assessments or unit tests can be taken into account as well. Teachers may also suggest additional factors to consider as evidence of student learning, such as student portfolios or data that might be unique to a particular school.

> **Task 2 (Teaching and Learning, Assessment)**: Identify what evidence of student learning you will gather. Organize data to show how all groups within the school are performing across the full scope of the math program, including, if possible, students' ability to make connections among mathematical topics for solving in-depth or extended problems.

Whatever student data are gathered, it's important to disaggregate the data to look at performance of various groups of students, including racial and socioeconomic groups as well as English language learners and special education students. If any group's performance is significantly lower than the school's performance overall, it's important to ask whether those students are being given the same opportunity to learn as other students. Differences in performance can sometimes point to structural problems in a school, such as inequitable tracking practices or pull-out programs that limit the scope of mathematics a student is exposed to. On the surface, it may seem that such practices allow teachers to target students' individual needs. But research continues to verify that tracking practices do not serve students well (Burris et al., 2009; Oakes & Saunders, 2008). And in too many cases, students of color and students coming from poverty are likely to be disproportionately, and often inappropriately, represented in lower tracks or groups. If a stranger can walk down the hallway of a school and identify the level of a class just by looking in the doorway, there may be a problem with student placement (Seeley, 2015). Ideally, the demographics of every classroom should reflect the demographics of the school. One charter school I visited a few years ago has two classes at each grade level, and the school makes a practice of regrouping students at the end of the first semester if the two groups' grades or test scores are too different. The leaders of the school believe that maintaining heterogeneity and high expectations for every class is essential in order for all students to perform at the highest level possible.

Data on program structure. It's important to look at the content and organization of the math program—as defined by state standards, reflected in curriculum documents and instructional materials, and implemented in the classroom.

Task 3 (Content, Habits of Mind): Look at how content evolves across the grades as described in standards and grade or course curriculum documents. Consider whether the content balances concepts, computation, and problem solving. Notice how well mathematical practices and mathematical thinking are developed. Have priority topics been identified for each grade or course? Examine instructional materials to verify their alignment with program goals and determine how well they reflect appropriate learning trajectories across grades or courses for priority topics.

Task 4 (Content, Habits of Mind, Teachers, Teaching and Learning): Compare the demographic makeup of individual classes to the demographics of the school and note whether all students are given opportunities to learn the full breadth of mathematics offered in the program. Identify examples of potentially inequitable practices, such as students being tracked or pulled out of math class to work on lower-level skills.

Data on teachers and teaching. Teachers represent the heart of any math program, so it can be informative to evaluate their knowledge and background. This task is not as straightforward as looking at college transcripts to see how many math credits each teacher has accumulated. Some teachers have earned many credits in mathematics or have a major or minor in the subject. Others may have invested heavily in their own learning once they began teaching. Still others may come to teaching as a second career, bringing strong quantitative skills and experience from their previous work. The most important factor may well be whether a teacher is continuing to learn and grow, through formal study or perhaps through experiences within the school community such as participating in a worthwhile professional learning community or engaging in a lesson study process with colleagues.

Data on what kind of teaching is going on in classrooms day to day can best be gathered through direct observation (e.g., from classroom walk-throughs or videotaped lessons). The most effective approach involves consultation with the teacher that includes discussion before and debriefing after an observation. It's important to realize that effective teaching of mathematics may not necessarily involve the same strategies or structure as effective teaching in other disciplines. Any instruments or tools used in classroom observation should be designed to look for factors important to deep mathematics learning, including whether students are developing thinking skills, solving complex problems, and making sense of numbers and operations. Gathering this kind of information can be one of the most time-consuming parts of taking stock of your math program, but it can also provide some of the most powerful insights as to how students are learning—or why they may not be learning as much as they could. Teacher evaluation systems are expected to incorporate multiple observations and other measures, in light of expectations in the Every Student Succeeds Act of 2015. One possible tool for addressing such expectations in math and science is a system called the Surveys of Enacted Curriculum, developed by the Council of Chief State School Officers and the Wisconsin Center for Educational Research (WCER, 2015).

Task 5 (Teachers): Conduct a scan of teachers' math backgrounds in terms of both coursework and professional learning outside of a college or university setting.

Task 6 (Teachers, Teaching and Learning): Gather observation data about how classrooms operate, focusing on whether all students have the opportunity to wrestle with challenging, relevant problems; engage in productive struggle toward meaning, understanding, and proficiency; discuss their strategies and answers with each other; and make sense of the mathematics they're learning.

Task 7 (Teacher Evaluation): Examine your teacher evaluation system to determine how well it recognizes and rewards effective mathematics teaching for depth, understanding, and proficiency.

Data on school climate and outreach. A school's mathematics program needs to be considered within the context of the school as a whole, including other school priorities, outside initiatives, and the overall environment of the school.

Task 8 (Teaching and Learning, Outreach): Identify what other programs and initiatives teachers of mathematics are dealing with that might influence the time they spend planning or teaching mathematics or that might push them in directions contrary to what they believe is best for their students. Ask teachers and other staff, as well as students and families, how they think the school leadership and staff view mathematics (e.g., as a high priority, useful, fun, something to celebrate, etc.).

Next Steps

Gathering the information needed to evaluate your mathematics program makes it possible to work with teachers and other stakeholders to build on what seems to be working or shows promise, while also addressing those areas that may need improvement. Unless a program is completely failing, it's generally preferable to target particular areas of need than to throw out a program altogether and create or bring in something new. If you determine that your program is in need of a comprehensive overhaul (which is beyond the scope of this book), it may be helpful to engage the help of one or more experts, such as partners at a nearby university or consultants at a regional service provider (Pelfrey, 2006; WCER, 2015).

How Do We Move from Ideas to Results?

If your school needs to work on one or more aspects of its mathematics program, consider the following general suggestions for dealing with and facilitating change.

Invest in Teachers

Teachers are the most important players in the mathematics education of students, and investing in their ongoing learning and day-to-day support generally yields positive results. Such an investment might involve organizing professional learning opportunities; providing additional resources that teachers request; scheduling time in the daily and yearly schedule for planning, meeting, and learning; and so on. Supporting teachers with math coaches can also be an excellent investment, providing a personal resource for teachers to help them refine their practice.

Rely on Your Math Experts

If your district has a math coordinator or supervisor, or if your school has math coaches or designated department heads or math team leads, consider asking these individuals to assume leadership roles in both planning and working with teachers. If you don't have access to such experts, research what resources are available from the district, region, or state or consult faculty members at a nearby college or university. And don't forget to look for experts among your school or district's own mathematics teachers. Professional math teachers with a solid knowledge of their field and expertise in teaching can also be considered as potential local experts to help guide or lead improvement efforts.

Create Opportunities for Collaboration

Teachers' most precious resource is time, and finding ways to offer time to take part in important planning activities within a level or across levels can be a tremendous gift, if used well. There's a thin line, however, between offering time and taking time. Simply fitting one more activity into an already packed professional development day, for example, may not prove fruitful and may add to teachers' stress. But if genuine planning or professional learning with colleagues takes place, that opportunity can build bridges and serve as a powerful stimulus for growth that continues from year to year.

Protect Your Teachers

Many school leaders are experts at deflecting external influences on their teachers. To the extent possible, work to keep outside (or your own) initiatives from interfering with day-to-day teaching and learning. Filter unnecessary initiatives or speak up to reject the one that might just be one too many. Insist that all programs and initiatives complement one another and fit with your teachers' ongoing work without intruding or interrupting learning.

Understand the Change Process

A leader is, of necessity, a change facilitator. And where improvement is called for, change is inevitable. In the role of change facilitator, it's important to remember some basic principles about how change takes place. Here are a few key reminders of what we know about facilitating change (for more in-depth resources about leadership and change, see the Encore section).

Change takes time. Change is a process, not an event. A major change takes time to succeed, even though leaders don't always have the luxury of providing as much time as we might like. But to the extent possible, identify ambitious but reachable goals, and establish a reasonable time line for planning and implementing any new program or initiative, even if it's only a modification to an existing program. The larger the expected change, the more modest should be the scale and time line for the change (Seeley, 2014). In addition, adequate funding and ongoing support for teachers are essential for any program. Most of all, make a commitment to stay the course long enough, typically years, to see results. If (when) inevitable problems arise, make a commitment to fine-tune, not throw out, the program.

Involve stakeholders early. Teachers are generally the ones expected to bear the bulk of the responsibility for implementing a new initiative. Accordingly, they should be represented in the planning process and consulted regularly throughout implementation. But others may also have a stake in what happens, including students and parents or other community members. Consider involving

FIGURE 1: Stages of Concern, Concerns-Based Adoption Model

Stage of Concern	Typical Statement
0: Unconcerned	"I think I heard something about it, but I'm too busy right now with other priorities to be concerned about it."
1: Informational	"This seems interesting, and I would like to know more about it."
2: Personal	"I'm concerned about the changes I'll need to make in my routines."
3: Management	"I'm concerned about how much time it takes to get ready to teach with this new approach."
4: Consequence	"How will this new approach affect my students?"
5: Collaboration	"I'm looking forward to sharing some ideas about it with other teachers."
6: Refocusing	"I have some ideas about something that would work even better."

Source: SEDL, 2016.

representatives of all affected groups in the planning process and periodically as advisors.

Offer the right intervention at the right time. From some of the most useful research ever conducted on change, we know that people go through predictable stages as they implement anything new. Among other tools and resources, the Concerns-Based Adoption Model (CBAM, Hall & Hord, 2014) offers an extremely helpful description of seven "Stages of Concern" that people are likely to move through as they undertake a new initiative (see Figure 1).

If we are aware of these stages, we can tailor appropriate interventions to be optimally helpful for wherever an individual or group may be in the change process. When I was working as a brand-new district math coordinator and studying the CBAM model in graduate school, I was responsible for guiding the adoption of a districtwide K–12 objectives-based mathematics program, so my coursework was particularly relevant to my day-to-day work. We had ensured that teachers participated in in-depth professional development prior to the beginning of the school year, and I was in schools every day to offer assistance. Unsurprisingly, though, a few months into our implementation efforts, people seemed to be unsettled, frustrated, or worse. I discussed with a colleague who was also in my graduate class how we might proceed. How could we offer the right kind of assistance to teachers? Did they need another workshop on some aspect of the program? Were they lacking any potentially useful materials? Could they benefit from more planning time? We decided to find out what the teachers were most concerned about—where they were in the change process in terms of the Stages of Concern.

I organized a series of after-school meetings in each of the eight schools in the district. I brought food to each meeting, and made sure teachers could settle in and have a snack before we started. I posted two large sheets of poster paper and told the teachers that everyone would have a chance to share their concerns. One by one, they were asked to identify one thing they were unhappy about, and I recorded these items on one sheet of paper. But they were also asked to identify one thing they liked about the program; I recorded these items on the other sheet of paper. We went around the room until no one had anything else to contribute. I grouped together similar concerns to make a summary chart of what people wanted, needed, or were worried about, and we then talked about how we might address that issue.

In some cases, this simple exercise resulted in someone sharing something positive that addressed a concern or need someone else had. In other cases, I was able to determine what intervention or assistance might be most helpful. Predictably, most people seemed to be at Stage 2, concerned on a Personal level ("This is so hard"; "I'm not sure I can handle this"; "What if I don't do it right?"). For those people, having someone listen to their concern, and hearing that others shared it, helped defuse their worry—and I then knew how to support them. Over the next several weeks, I made sure to take time when teachers weren't with students to listen to them and see how they were feeling. A few teachers were past that point and at Stage 3, concerned with Management issues ("I need help organizing the materials"; "The record-keeping form is confusing"). I also knew what those individuals needed, and subsequently, the issues raised about the record-keeping form led us to make a small revision that helped everyone.

The most important lesson for me from this experience (and from many experiences since then) is that any intervention is useful only if it offers what someone needs at about the time they need it. If we don't identify where people are in the process, we're likely to waste time and money on a workshop or additional materials that aren't needed and will still leave people frustrated. Determining and then offering a more appropriate intervention, such as an opportunity to talk through personal concerns, might be far more effective at a certain time for certain individuals. Later in the implementation, that same workshop or materials—offered when there is an identified need—can result in significant positive results.

What Should I Watch Out For?

The road to a better math program is full of potholes. We can anticipate some of them, but others will catch us by surprise. What may be most important to keep in mind is to try to avoid surprises for the people on the front line (usually teachers) and focus on long-range goals. Along the way, we can predict that some or all of the following issues might appear.

The Fad *du Jour*

Anyone who has been involved in education for even a few years has likely experienced the arrival (and often departure) of a new trend or fad (Seeley, 2015). It may be a lesson planning model (e.g., Madeline Hunter's formulaic lesson plan), a teaching approach (e.g., the 5E Instructional Model for science), a test preparation program designed exactly for the standards you just adopted (too many to mention, often available before the program they allegedly address is finalized), or any of hundreds of other kinds of programs, many of which seem to appear almost overnight. Unfortunately, many fads turn out to be little more than superficial ideas blown out of proportion. Far too often, schools spend large amounts of money to implement something that may not even fit their needs. And in many cases, they don't plan well in advance or support the implementation over time.

Sometimes a trend may be a true innovation that is easily transportable to a situation other than the one in which it was developed and helpful to teachers. The 5E Instructional Model for science teaching is one such long-standing example. Developed by BSCS in the 1980s (Bybee et al., 2006), this model advocates incorporating five basic steps into science lessons (Engage, Explore, Explain, Elaborate, and Evaluate). These components help teachers understand what's involved in a rich science lesson, and the model seems to be readily adapted for many classrooms. But not all good ideas work well in all contexts. An idea that works well in one situation may not be the solution in a different school or if used for a purpose other than the one it was created for. And even a well-conceived idea needs adequate planning and support in order to be successfully implemented.

In general, it's wise to be cautious about any program or resource that seems to have caught on overnight—and especially wary if a program has only been around for a short time. If a resource truly fits your program and purposes and will help teachers and students, then it is worth spending time on a thorough examination and review of the resource by teachers and others who may be affected by it, including taking a hard look at results in places where the program has been used. I was once asked to visit a district to see if I could explain why their middle school test results had plummeted. It quickly became obvious that the adoption of a commercial program in grades 3–5—a suddenly popular test preparation program that had taken root throughout the region near the school and was touted as a surefire way to prepare students to ace their state accountability test—had led to unexpected problems. The program had limited math instruction so severely in the elementary grades that it effectively eroded the foundation students needed in middle school in order to develop a deep understanding of proportional relationships and basic algebraic reasoning. The district had adopted the elementary program without considering how it fit within their overall program, especially in terms of developing critical learning trajectories across grades for important strands in mathematics. While they initially saw some short-term gains at grades 3, 4, and 5, those gains flattened in the second year of the program, and scores started dropping in successive grades almost immediately.

Resistance from Teachers

Some teachers are reluctant to change their practice or adopt a new approach. It's hard to blame them; many have seen one program after another come and go over the years. They may have come to think that it's not worth investing their time and energy into "this New Thing" when they are likely to see it quickly pass and be replaced by "the next New Thing."

The best way to prevent resistance from teachers is to establish a history and culture of well-thought-out program advances accompanied by support and long-term commitment. If a leader inherits teachers who have been through the opposite experience, involving them directly in the planning and implementation process may be the best way to head off resistance. Beyond that, it may be helpful to rely on using what we know about how people deal with change, such as the Stages of Concern from the Concerns-Based Adoption Model, to determine how to best support teachers in ways they recognize and appreciate.

There may be times when it's best not to focus on the few teachers who are resisting, and instead invest in and celebrate the accomplishments of those who are fully engaged. Sometimes their energy will overcome their colleagues' resistance. In extreme cases of resistance or refusal to do what is expected, it may be necessary to encourage a teacher to look for a more suitable school.

Resistance from Parents or the Community

At times, parents may not understand the changes a school undertakes in their children's math program. If their students have previously been successful in math, and their grades start dropping, parents may be particularly concerned and may become vocal opponents of the changes. It's important to address parent concerns as early and constructively as possible, especially in terms of communicating the broad goal of raising the level of mathematical thinking for all students, including their own. Ideally, one or more carefully selected parents can be involved in some level of planning a change or new element to the school's math program.

Teachers and other staff members can also be helpful in heading off parent or community concerns. A lot of community outreach can take place within the context of what I call "grocery line conversation." When teachers engage in casual conversation with friends or neighbors who are parents, they can generate much support or do great harm without even realizing it. A teacher saying to someone outside the school setting, "I'm really excited about the great things my students are doing now that we've started focusing on problem solving!" is likely to achieve a very different result from one who says, "You won't believe what they're making me do now!" Remind teachers of the power of their offhand remarks to people who may only hear the headline and miss the details.

If you can identify community members who are knowledgeable about what you're trying to accomplish, you might encourage them to share what they know with friends. They might write letters to the local newspaper or to the school board expressing support. I have a friend who's a computer scientist at a major university. She frequently volunteers in her children's schools and has served on various committees related to K–12 education, and she recently started writing a monthly column on education for her small local newspaper. Enlisting the help of such a supporter can go a long way toward overcoming people's natural resistance to change, especially if the support comes from a professional in a related field from within their community.

Yo-Yo Decision Making

Finally, the worst thing we do in education—the thing that kills more good ideas, demoralizes more teachers, and interferes with more learning than anything else we do—is what I call *yo-yo decision making*. This all-too-common phenomenon usually involves spending immense amounts of money and asking for significant work on the part of teachers to implement a new program, only to abandon the program before it's had a chance to succeed. Often, the impetus for abandoning the program is so that a different program can be implemented, perhaps also requiring immense amounts of money and significant work on the part of teachers. Teachers are essentially pulled in one direction, only to be jerked back in another direction, often within a period of just a year or two—and sometimes even more quickly than that.

Any new program is likely to encounter some difficulties that call for adjustments. Such adjustments are perfectly normal, and they can almost always be implemented in a way that helps the program continue toward success. Nobody benefits, however, if we can't build on work done this year to go further next year, and the year after that, and the year after that. We lose momentum and progress when we yank the rug out from under teachers and students by changing the rules and priorities year after year.

As a leader, try to avoid falling into the trap of imposing yo-yo decision making on your teachers. Plan well and support your new program. When things get tough, look for how to resolve issues without jumping ship. Work to make whatever adjustments may be necessary. Involve key stakeholders. Address concerns. Unless overwhelming evidence shows that the program is hurting students, reaffirm your commitment to do whatever it takes to support the program and let it work. And do what you can to prevent others from inflicting their own yo-yo decision making on the teachers you work with.

Conclusion

Making a math program work is an ambitious task, but it is also one of the most important tasks a leader can undertake. If we do our job well, we can produce students who can think mathematically and use what they know to solve problems—even problems that don't look like the word problems at the end of the chapter. The central players in making any initiative work are teachers, and the key to success is equipping them to create classrooms where students are constantly engaged in the process of wrestling with complex problems and discussing their thinking on the path to learning important and useful skills and concepts. Effective leaders can multiply the effects of individual teachers by creating opportunities for collaboration and planning within and across grades and levels. An effective leader, working together with teachers, can build a positive math culture that supports a program with the depth, substance, and continuity to help every student become a mathematically proficient problem solver.

To give your feedback on this publication and
be entered into a drawing for a free ASCD
Arias e-book, please visit
www.ascd.org/ariasfeedback

ASCD | arias™

ENCORE

WHAT CAN WE DO?

The most important purpose of this book is to stimulate action. Whether you want to refine an already successful program or consider a major redirection, the questions below might provide a starting point. To help you identify next steps, I suggest reflecting on these questions, either individually or in discussion with others. Consider the resources listed at the end of this section as you use the results of your reflections and discussions to develop a plan for examining and refining or redirecting your mathematics program.

Reflection/Discussion

- What Does It Mean to Be Good at Math?
    - How much do you and your teachers know about a growth mindset? How can you learn more?
    - How can an understanding of a growth mindset and what it means to be smart in math help your school or district better meet the needs of all students, including those who might be marginalized in remedial or special classes?
- What Should a Good Mathematics Program Look Like?
    - How well does your math program reflect a balance of—and connections among—concepts, computation, and problem solving? Which area(s) might you need to strengthen?

— How broad or limited is your school's approach to developing mathematical fluency? Does your school have a policy regarding timed tests? If so, how well does it support the development of students' positive disposition toward mathematics?

— How well does your program address the full breadth of what it means to be mathematically proficient?

— How well does your program prepare students to be creative, innovative, and collaborative problem solvers, as needed for their future study and employment?

• How Do I Recognize, Support, and Evaluate Effective Math Teaching?

— In what ways do you support teachers in becoming more knowledgeable about mathematics and how to teach it? What other avenues for professional learning might be available? How can you bring such options to your teachers?

— How well do you utilize productive professional learning communities as a vehicle for supporting teachers and improving mathematics teaching and learning? How can you create or strengthen the use of professional learning communities in your school?

— In what ways do your school policies support or interfere with teachers teaching in meaningful, lasting ways? What adjustments might be called for?

— How well do your hiring and staffing practices ensure that every student is taught mathematics by a teacher who knows and likes the subject?

— How well does your teacher evaluation system recognize and reward problem-focused, student-centered teaching (upside-down teaching)? What adjustments might be called for?

- What's Working and What's Not?
  — In which of the seven components of a high-quality math program (Content, Habits of Mind, Teachers, Teaching and Learning, Assessment, Teacher Evaluation, Outreach) do you think you are strongest? Which areas might need attention?

  — How much change are you willing to consider if the evidence dictates a need for improvement? What resources can you make available (people, money, time, etc.) in support of any improvement effort?

  — What would be a good first step in taking stock of your math program to determine what's working and what's not? Who can you involve at this initial stage in order to generate the best information and to engage potential stakeholders?

  — What sources of data or evidence do you have available? What other types of data not currently available might you be able to obtain?

- — How will you identify possible next steps, and who can you involve to help you determine what might be needed or helpful?
- How Do We Move from Ideas to Results?
  - — What kinds of investments in teachers might offer the greatest payoff in terms of short- and long-term improvement in mathematics teaching and learning?
  - — Who are the math experts in your school, district, or community? How can you involve these experts as partners in any process you undertake to support or improve your mathematics program?
  - — What opportunities do you create for collaboration about mathematics within and across grade levels and courses? Are there other ways to enhance continuity and coherence from grade to grade and school to school?
  - — How effective are you at protecting your teachers from external influences that might interfere with their teaching effectiveness?
  - — How well do you understand the change process? How can you learn more?
- What Should I Watch Out For?
  - — What potential fads might you be implementing or considering for your school or district? How might you either rethink or build adequate support for such efforts?

— As you think about new directions or initiatives you might like to undertake, how willing are you to commit to building an infrastructure that will increase the likelihood of lasting success?

— How might you minimize resistance from teachers, parents, and community members if you plan to make changes in your math program?

— To what extent are you willing to make a long-term commitment to support whatever program refinements or changes you might undertake? How strong is your commitment to avoiding yo-yo decision making?

Resources for Taking Stock of a Math Program

National Council of Teachers of Mathematics. (2011). *Teacher evaluation*. Position statement. Reston, VA: Author.

National Council of Teachers of Mathematics. (2014). *Principles to actions: Ensuring mathematical success for all*. Reston, VA: Author.

Pelfrey, R. (2006). *The mathematics program improvement review: A comprehensive evaluation process for K–12 schools*. Alexandria, VA: ASCD.

Wisconsin Center for Education Research. (2015). Surveys of enacted curriculum. Retrieved from https://secure.wceruw.org/seconline/secwebhome.htm

Resources on Facilitating Change

Benson, J. (2015). *10 steps to managing change in schools: How do we take initiatives from goals to actions?* (ASCD Arias) Alexandria, VA: ASCD.

Fullan, M. (2007). *Leading in a culture of change*. San Francisco: Jossey-Bass.

Hall, G. E., & Hord, S. M. (2014). *Implementing change: Patterns, principles, and potholes* (4th ed.). Boston: Allyn & Bacon.

References

Boaler, J. (2015). *Mathematical mindsets: Unleashing students' potential through creative math, inspiring messages and innovative teaching.* San Francisco: Jossey-Bass.

Burris, C. C., Welner, K. G., & Bezoza, J. W. (2009). *Universal access to a quality education: Research and recommendations for the elimination of curricular stratification.* Boulder, CO: Education and the Public Interest Center, University of Colorado; and Tempe, AZ: Education Policy Research Unit, Arizona State University. Retrieved from http://nepc.colorado.edu/files/Epic-Epru_LB-UnivAcc-FINAL.pdf

Bybee, R. W., Taylor, J. A., Gardner, A., Van Scotter, P., Powell, J. C., Westbrook, A., & Landes, N. (2006). *The BSCS 5E Instructional Model: Origins, effectiveness and applications, executive summary.* Colorado Springs, CO: BSCS. Retrieved from http://www.bscs.org/sites/default/files/_legacy/BSCS_5E_Instructional_Model-Executive_Summary_0.pdf

Chapin, S. H., O'Connor, C., & Anderson, N. C. (2013). *Classroom discussions in math: A teacher's guide for using talk moves to support the Common Core and more, grades K–6* (3rd ed.). Sausalito, CA: Math Solutions.

The Charles A. Dana Center at the University of Texas at Austin. (2016). Academic Youth Development [Website]. Retrieved from http://utdanacenter.org/ayd

Dweck, C. S. (2006). *Mindset: The new psychology of success.* New York: Ballantine Books.

Every Student Succeeds Act, S.1177, 114th Cong. (2015).

Findell, B., & Swafford, J. (Eds.). (2002). *Helping children learn mathematics.* Washington, DC: National Academy Press.

Fisher, D., & Frey, N. (2013). *Better learning through structured teaching: A framework for the gradual release of responsibility* (2nd ed.). Alexandria, VA: ASCD.

Hall, G. E., & Hord, S. M. (2014). *Implementing change: Patterns, principles and potholes* (4th ed.). Boston: Allyn & Bacon.

Mathematical Association of America, Committee on the Undergraduate Program in Mathematics. (2015). *2015 CUPM curriculum guide to majors in the mathematical sciences.* Retrieved from http://www.maa.org/programs/faculty-and-departments/curriculum-department-guidelines-recommendations/cupm

National Council of Teachers of Mathematics. (2011). *Teacher evaluation.* Position statement. Reston, VA: Author.

National Council of Teachers of Mathematics. (2014a). *Principles to actions: Ensuring mathematical success for all.* Reston, VA: Author.

National Council of Teachers of Mathematics. (2014b). *Procedural fluency in mathematics.* Position statement. Reston, VA: Author.

National Council of Teachers of Mathematics & Council for the Accreditation of Educator Preparation. (2012). *NCTM CAEP standards (2012).* Retrieved from http://www.nctm.org/ncate/

Oakes, J., & Saunders, M. (Eds.). (2008). *Beyond tracking: Multiple pathways to college, career, and civic participation.* Cambridge, MA: Harvard Education Press.

Pearson, P. D., & Gallagher, M. (1983). The instruction of reading comprehension. *Contemporary Educational Psychology, 8*(3), 317–344.

Pelfrey, R. (2006). *The mathematics program improvement review: A comprehensive evaluation process for K–12 schools.* Alexandria, VA: ASCD.

SEDL. (2016). Stages of concern [Webpage]. Retrieved from https://www.sedl.org/cbam/stages_of_concern.html

Seeley, C. L. (2014). *Smarter than we think: More messages about math, teaching, and learning in the 21st century.* Sausalito, CA: Math Solutions.

Seeley, C. L. (2015). *Faster isn't smarter: Messages about math, teaching, and learning in the 21st century* (2nd ed.). Sausalito, CA: Math Solutions.

Seeley, C. L. (2016). *Making sense of math: How to help every student become a mathematical thinker and problem solver.* Alexandria, VA: ASCD.

Smith, M. S., & Stein, M. K. (2011). *5 practices for orchestrating mathematics discussions.* Reston, VA: National Council of Teachers of Mathematics.

Wisconsin Center for Education Research. (2015). Surveys of enacted curriculum. Retrieved from https://secure.wceruw.org/seconline/secwebhome.htm

Related ASCD Resources

At the time of publication, the following ASCD resources were available (ASCD stock numbers appear in parentheses). For up-to-date information about ASCD resources, go to www.ascd.org. You can search the complete archives of *Educational Leadership* at http://www.ascd.org/el.

ASCD EDge®
Exchange ideas and connect with other educators interested in math on the social networking site ASCD EDge at http://ascdedge.ascd.org.

Print Products
From Standards to Success: A Guide for School Leaders by Mark R. O'Shea (#105017)

Habits of Mind Across the Curriculum: Practical and Creative Strategies for Teachers by Arthur L. Costa & Bena Kallick (#108014)

Making Sense of Math: How to Help Every Student Become a Mathematical Thinker and Problem Solver (ASCD Arias) by Cathy L. Seeley (#SF116067)

The Mathematics Program Improvement Review: A Comprehensive Evaluation Process for K–12 Schools by Ron Pelfrey (#105126)

School Climate Change: How do I build a positive environment for learning? (ASCD Arias) by Peter DeWitt & Sean Slade (#SF114084)

STEM Leadership: How do I create a STEM culture in my school? (ASCD Arias) by Traci Buckner & Brian Boyd (#SF114081)

10 Steps to Managing Change in Schools: How do we take initiatives from goals to actions? (ASCD Arias) by Jeffrey Benson (#SF115072)

For more information: send e-mail to member@ascd.org; call 1-800-933-2723 or 703-578-9600, press 2; send a fax to 703-575-5400; or write to Information Services, ASCD, 1703 N. Beauregard St., Alexandria, VA 22311-1714 USA.

About the Author

Cathy Seeley is committed to high-quality mathematics for every student. She has worked as a teacher, district mathematics coordinator, and Texas state mathematics director for grades K–12 and is a sought-after speaker, having spoken in all 50 states and around the world. After returning in late 2001 from teaching mathematics (in French) as a Peace Corps volunteer in Burkina Faso, Cathy was elected to serve as President of the National Council of Teachers of Mathematics. In that role, she received an EXCEL Gold Award for her President's Message "Embracing Accountability." She has appeared on television and radio and authored or coauthored various publications including textbooks. Her book *Faster Isn't Smarter: Messages About Math, Teaching, and Learning in the 21st Century* received a 2010 AEP Distinguished Achievement Award. It was followed in 2014 by the publication of *Smarter Than We Think: More Messages About Math, Teaching, and Learning in the 21st Century*. Cathy recently retired as a Senior Fellow with the Charles A. Dana Center at the University of Texas, where she worked on state and national policy and improvement efforts, with a focus on prekindergarten–grade 12 mathematics. Visit Cathy's website at www.cathyseeley.com.

WHOLE CHILD
TENETS

1 **HEALTHY**
Each student enters school healthy and learns about and practices a healthy lifestyle.

2 **SAFE**
Each student learns in an environment that is physically and emotionally safe for students and adults.

3 **ENGAGED**
Each student is actively engaged in learning and is connected to the school and broader community.

4 **SUPPORTED**
Each student has access to personalized learning and is supported by qualified, caring adults.

5 **CHALLENGED**
Each student is challenged academically and prepared for success in college or further study and for employment and participation in a global environment.

ASCD's Whole Child approach is an effort to transition from a focus on narrowly defined academic achievement to one that promotes the long-term development and success of all children. Through this approach, ASCD supports educators, families, community members, and policymakers as they move from a vision about educating the whole child to sustainable, collaborative actions.

Building a Math-Positive Culture: How to Support Great Math Teaching in Your School relates to the **engaged, supported,** and **challenged** tenets.

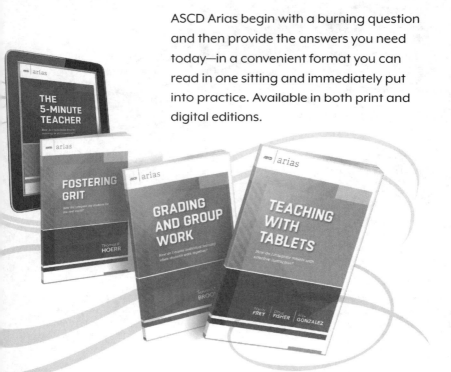